MEDITATIONS ON THE BEATITUDES

MEDITATIONS ON THE BEATITUDES

Lessons from the Margins

Donald R. Clymer

Foreword by
Leanne Eshleman Benner

Publishing House
Telford, Pennsylvania

Cascadia Publishing House LLC orders, information, reprint permissions:
contact@cascadiapublishinghouse.com
1-215-723-9125
126 Klingerman Road, Telford PA 18969
www.CascadiaPublishingHouse.com

Meditations on the Beatitudes
Copyright © 2011 by Cascadia Publishing House
a division of Cascadia Publishing House LLC, Telford, PA
18969
All rights reserved.
Library of Congress Catalog Number: 2011007355
ISBN 13: 978-1-931038-85-0; **ISBN 10:** 1-931038-85-6
Book design by Cascadia Publishing House
Cover design by Dawn Ranck

The paper used in this publication is recycled and meets the minimum requirements of American National Standard for Information Sciences—Permanence of Paper for Printed Library Materials, ANSI Z39.48-1984.

All Bible quotations are used by permission, all rights reserved and unless otherwise noted are from *The New Revised Standard Version of the Bible*, copyright 1989, by the Division of Christian Education of the National Council of the Churches of Christ in the USA

Library of Congress Cataloguing-in-Publication Data
Clymer, Donald R., 1948-
  Meditations on the beatitudes : lessons from the margins / Donald R. Clymer.
   p. cm.
  Includes bibliographical references.
  Summary: "What does it mean to be meek? To hunger and thirst after righteousness? The author draws on stories from years of experience in Latin America to invite readers to glean nsights regarding the Beatitudes' meaning." "[summary]"--Provided by publisher.
  ISBN-13: 978-1-931038-85-0 (5.5 x 8.5 trade pbk. : alk. paper)
  ISBN-10: 1-931038-85-6 (5.5 x 8.5 trade pbk. : alk. paper)
  1. Beatitudes--Criticism, interpretation, etc. 2. Christianity--Latin America. I. Title.

BT382.C59 2011
226.9'306--dc22

2011007355

20 19 18 17 16 15 13 12 11   10 9 8 7 6 5 4 3 2 1

To
my wife Esther,
who has been a constant and consistent companion through many struggles with cultural, biblical, and personal understandings.

Without her steadfastness and support, my journey through life would have been much more fraught with troubles.

CONTENTS

Foreword by Leanne Eshleman Benner   9
Acknowledgments   11
Introduction   13

Beatitude 1 • 21
Beatitude 2 • 27
Beatitude 3 • 32
Beatitude 4 • 37
Beatitude 5 • 43
Beatitude 6 • 49
Beatitude 7 • 55
Beatitude 8 • 61
Beatitude 9 • 66
Beatitude 10 • 71

Notes   77
Bibliography   79
The Author   81

Foreword

I'm always taken aback when something like Don Clymer's book jolts me into realizing just how enmeshed I have become in a culture which barely needs the Beatitudes. Our pockets and our minds are full to overflowing. Reading the Beatitudes then becomes a sort of academic exercise and/or a checklist for making us feel better about ourselves.

Clymer vividly defines the Beatitudes through approaches that open new circuits of thought. Because of the way he interweaves other cultures into the picture, he helps us recognize our cultural blinders and encourages us to take them off. Clymer's passionate insights override the miasmic spirituality of a prosperous society. The poignant stories which begin each chapter abruptly shift us out of our comfort zones, much like when someone jumps off the other end of a see-saw. Suddenly we force-land and take a long, hard look at what just happened.

My hunger and thirst for righteousness grew the further I went in the book. I found myself a sort of "Zaccheus"—wanting to rush ahead to climb a tree and actually *see* Jesus. Each chapter focuses on one of the Beatitudes along with a story which in each case shed new light for me. Living the

Beatitudes, as Clymer puts it, teaches us "to walk in the light of Christ and . . . transform our impure impulses into life-giving action." I welcomed the invitations to explore my own heart and experiences to understand those areas in which I need enlightenment, confession, or healing. The meditations invite all of us to "come down" and "dine" with the Holy Spirit who can change our course.

Clymer's meditative style gives us ample time to truly explore our inner spirits where we, like him, have concocted a safe world for ourselves. His deeply personal and honest reflections give us permission to look at ourselves with the same depth of scrutiny he uses and not be overcome by what we find. I am struck by the intensity of feelings he brings to this study. Just when I feel like I need to come up for air, he suddenly opens the door to immense gratitude—despite confusion or frustration or hopelessness. It feels like a gift. And that, I think, is what the Beatitudes are all about!

Clymer's life-changing experiences are evident in his everyday life and not just on paper. We have walked together as church friends for years, and I have witnessed his ability to live with the discomfort and frustration of knowing several cultures very well and being able to move back and forth between them. That has its hurdles, and yet he continues to accept the challenge of loving we "middle-classers" and educating a whole new generation of students who pick up the truths of the Beatitudes more from his actions than his words.

Exploring the Beatitudes at an intercultural level lends a measure of hope and joy in the human resiliency which God has instilled in his children all over the world. If we are special, it is not because of our uniquenesses but our sameness with even the most broken and wretched of the earth. This book delves into that mystery and helps us take it to heart.

—*Leanne Eshleman Benner, Harrisonburg, Virginia, works at Virginia Mennonite Retirement Community as a Resident Services Manager*

ACKNOWLEDGMENTS

Many people have provided valuable assistance to me in writing this book. It made its first appearance as a project for a class on the book of Matthew at Eastern Mennonite Seminary. Without the critique and encouragement of professor Dorothy Jean Weaver, the manuscript probably would have become another archived, forgotten project.

For evaluating Latin American themes, Mennonite Central Committee (MCC) colleagues from Eastern Mennonite University (EMU), Jim and Ann Hershberger read the document in various stages and provided valuable feedback as did Deryl Yoder-Bontrager, Latin America regional director of MCC. From an intercultural perspective, Beth Aracena, director of EMU's cross-cultural programs, Orv Gingerich and his colleague Ann Butwell of Augsburg College's Center for Global Education did the same.

The publication committee of the Anabaptist Center for Religion and Society (ACRS) at Eastern Mennonite University, especially Vernon Jantzi, John Fairfield, and Ray Gingerich, worked diligently at helping to hone the book's thrust and audience.

Finally, after a myriad of revisions, I am truly indebted to Leanne Benner for carefully reading the document for flow and clarity. Her suggestions proved to be invaluable. Jon Dutcher read the document for mechanical errors, and my sister, Sharon Clymer Landis gave me moral support throughout the process. I am also deeply indebted to and grateful for Michael A. King of Cascadia Publishing House and his untiring support of this project.

INTRODUCTION

USING THESE LESSONS FROM THE MARGINS

These meditations on the Beatitudes are intended for use with Sunday school classes and small groups or for individuals. They can also be used by leaders of cross-cultural groups for reflection or discussion on cultural values and how to integrate kingdom values into one's own life. Groups or individuals can use the guided prayer section as well. Cross-cultural leaders can use the meditation and guided prayer as either discussion questions or journal entries.

Each beatitude is treated in the following manner:

BEATITUDE
The Beatitude from Matthew 5 is stated.

STORY
I recount a story from my personal experience in Latin America that relates to the beatitude.

Reflection
I share my thoughts and reflections on the story and the beatitude.

Conflicting Cultural Values
This is a section on how conflicting cultural values look at differences between the values of the kingdom of God and the prevailing culture.

Becoming the Beatitude
This section is an attempt to integrate what I have learned from those at the margin in Latin America; how I have tried to take each beatitude seriously.

Meditation and Guided Prayer
This section leads the individual or group into a time of guided prayer, reflection, and meditation on the beatitude, the story, and the conflicting cultural values. They are arranged in the order of disorientation and orientation.

Encountering and Learning from Strangers

The Beatitudes in the fifth chapter of Matthew's Gospel are the introduction to Jesus' Sermon on the Mount. I have always been fascinated by their meaning. The people whom Jesus claims will inherit the kingdom of heaven (God) are often characters that have marched through my life in the poverty-stricken lands of Latin America—the poor, the oppressed, those on the bottom rung of their social ladders. These people seem to reflect the characteristics of Jesus' Beatitudes better than most of the middle class people with whom I associate from my own cultural background. My encounter with these *strangers* and their *strange* culture, opened up brand new understandings and insights.

At age nineteen, I was thrust out of my naive and insular world in rural Pennsylvania into the world of intercultural relationships and the poverty of a developing world. I had been drafted during the Vietnam War, had registered as a conscientious objector, and had fulfilled my obligation to the government by serving a two-and-half year stint with a Christian voluntary service/mission agency (now Eastern Mennonite Missions, Salunga, Pa.) in Honduras. Little did I know how profoundly this encounter with strangers would affect me and how much I would learn from them.

Meeting and interacting with strangers plunged me into confusion and disorientation. I discovered that there is no right or wrong culture. All cultures reflect God's beauty and intent for human interconnectedness, but at the same time, all cultures distort that beauty and intent. It was quite difficult for me to throw off the blinders of my U.S. American socialization and admit such a discovery. Nevertheless, I experienced God in startling new ways. Torn away from my cultural heritage, God seemed as alien and strange as the new culture in which I was immersed.

The intersection of this unfamiliar culture with its unfamiliar people and this new God, became the spawning ground of spiritual growth. What I thought was a fulfillment of an obligation to my government and, to a lesser extent to my faith, became a new understanding of God—a new spirituality. David Smith describes precisely my experience in his book *Learning From the Stranger*: "Intercultural learning is not just a means to a later end, but can itself be a process that encourages and involves spiritual growth."[1]

That process, however, did not happen without pain and struggle with my faith and identity. The strangers I refer to in the following stories were undoubtedly changed by their encounter with me as well. Nevertheless, I can only tell their stories from my particular perspective and world view—even if broadly expanded. My struggles with incorporating the values they taught me, given in more detail below, gave a sense of blessedness which only comes through a deep encounter with God and his creatures. Let's take a look now at the Beatitudes and their ensuing blessings.

INTRODUCTION TO THE BEATITUDES

There have been numerous attempts to get to the real meaning of the word *blessed* which appears at the beginning of each beatitude. In Greek the word used is *makarioi*.[2] The NRSV along with many other versions translate the word into a phrase—*blessed are*. Others render it *happy are*, or *fortunate are*.

As close as these renderings get to its true meaning, according to Douglas Hare in his book on Matthew, it is "difficult to find an adequate translation for the word."[3] William Barclay writes that in the phrase there actually "is no verb, [there] is no *are*."[4] It is more like a Hebrew expression Jesus would have known and used. This expression in Hebrew is *'esher*, as used in Psalm 1:1,[5] which Barclay thinks more accurately should be translated: "O the blessedness of."[6] Hare states: "It is . . . suggested that the original force of the word would be better captured in English by rendering it as 'congratulations.'"[7] Whatever the exact meaning is of *blessed* in the Beatitudes, the emphasis should be on the fact that, "Happiness derives from a right relationship with God."[8]

There have been numerous attempts to explain how the Sermon on the Mount and likewise the Beatitudes, apply or do not apply to our ethical behavior. Many would have us believe that the Sermon applies to some future age when Christ reigns over the earth. According to Providence Baptist Ministries' website, "[Some] have dwelt upon its dispensational bearings, insisting that it belongs not to the saints of the present dispensation but to believers within a future millennium."[9] Did Matthew write his Gospel, and, in particular, the Sermon on the Mount for some future generation? Or was it for his fledgling community that was battling the emerging formative Judaism?

Andrew Overman claims that "The Sermon is intended to instruct the Matthean community on how they are to act, treat one another, and order their internal affairs."[10] As such, "The opening Beatitudes describe in ideal terms the traits and characteristics of the members of the community."[11] If, as Overman insists, Matthew was writing these instructions as ethical guidelines for the life of the Matthean community, why would they *not* apply to the church of today?

Mark Powell writes this about the Beatitudes: "As the opening words of the Sermon on the Mount, these verses provide a foundation for understanding the core of Jesus' ethical instruction."[12] Furthermore, according to Barclay,

> It means that the Beatitudes are not pious hopes of what shall be; they are not glowing, but nebulous prophecies of some future bliss; they are *congratulations* on what is. The blessedness which belongs to the Christian is not a blessedness which is postponed to some future world of glory; it is a blessedness which exists here and now.[13]

The first four Beatitudes promise "eschatological reversals to those who are unfortunate,"[14] according to Powell. Those who are dispossessed here on earth will receive their reward in the fullness of time. Through no fault of their own they find themselves at the margin of society. The second set of Beatitudes promise "eschatological rewards to people who exhibit virtuous behavior."[15] These people exhibit the "greater righteousness" (Matt. 5:20) to which Jesus calls us; they are concerned with "the weightier matters of the law: justice and mercy" (Matt. 23:23). These are people who choose to go against the cultural flow and live at the margin of their society.

The ninth *blessed are* is not considered a beatitude by scholars because it does not follow the structure of the first eight and is given in the second person while the others are all in the third person. I have included it and added a tenth to have an even number of lessons for this meditation. The tenth beatitude is invented and taken from Matt. 19:30 and 20:16 because of its theme in the Gospel of Matthew as well as the theme of this study.

These devotional meditations were written with the view that they are meant as an ethical guide for living out our Christian faith in our world today, and that these ethical statements will often conflict with our cultural values.

Meditations on the Beatitudes

BEATITUDE 1

Matt. 5:3: *Blessed are the poor in spirit, for theirs is the kingdom of heaven.*

STORY

One Saturday in rural Mexico, I was invited to a meal in a small village by a man who had just received a home built by volunteers with Mennonite Central Committee (MCC). This was his way to celebrate his new home. The house was only a frame—no doors, no windows. In many such cases, MCC supplied the frame for the earthquake-resistant houses and each individual family provided the windows and doors as finances allowed. As a result, these homes sometimes took several years to complete. This day my wife and I were royally ushered inside and invited to relax on the only furnishings in the home—a few chairs and a table around an open dining room.

As we ate, chickens and other animals freely came and went around us, leaving droppings in various spots across the room. The food was delicious, and we used tortillas to protect our fingers from the spicy, savory sauces. My wife and I admired how happy our friend and his family were as they served us, despite the few material possessions they had.

The next day offered an entirely different experience. It was Sunday and I traveled to a nearby city and attended a local church. After the service my wife and I were invited to a factory owner's home for dinner with his family. Since he was from a German-speaking background like my wife, and went occasionally to the Lutheran church we attended while visiting in the city, we quickly became friends. We dined in his huge house, complete with exquisite decorations and a swimming pool. Five courses featuring European-quality cuisine were served on fine china and silver, with a maid attending to our every need. Despite all the pomp and glitter, the man's forehead was lined with deep wrinkles, suggesting many worries that preoccupied him.

REFLECTION

Two days. Two totally different worlds only a few miles apart. The juxtaposition of poverty and wealth tore at my soul. How could some people be born with silver spoons and others with only tortillas?

When I think of poverty, I normally think of the man in the first half of the story—who lacks material possessions and has limited access to goods and services. I seldom think of poverty of the soul. Yet the man in the second part of the story lacked in spirituality what the first man lacked in possessions. This rich man was lonely, cynical, and worried about the security of his family and all his possessions. This man was distracted and had little time for God. He depended on market forces, bribery, and nepotism rather than God. Wouldn't he fit the description of those who "gain the whole world but forfeit their life" (or "soul," as NIV puts it)? (Matt. 16:26). Matthew suggests that if he could admit to his poverty of soul, his being *poor in spirit*, he could be blessed.

In Luke's Gospel this beatitude reads, "Blessed are you who are poor" (Luke 6:20). What does the financially poor man in my story need in God's eyes? To be sure, he lacked even basic items to make his life a bit more comfortable; but for the most part, to my amazement, he conveyed the sense that he really had it made!

Without romanticizing the poor, this man taught me that a person can feel blessed even when far less in control of his life than would have suited me. He was dependent each day on God. He was grateful for each day of life that God had extended to him. He had time for his family and his friends. If he had any special needs, his neighbors and family banded together to help him. He had few cares or worries—no need for insurance to protect his investments and few material possessions worth stealing. This man experienced blessing because he centered his life around God's providence and not on his lack of material goods.

Donald Kraybill in *The Upside Down Kingdom* gives another sense of the phrase *poor in spirit*. These are the people whom we would call "poor souls"[16] in our culture. "Poor souls" are not necessarily those who have little money but, like most of the characters we will meet in this study, people who are pushed to the margins and looked down on by their culture. Interestingly enough, because of his myriad of worries about his wealth, the rich man in the story, despite what our culture thinks of his outward success, is a *poor soul*—a person to be pitied. Who of us wants to be a poor soul, a person to be pitied?

Conflicting Cultural Values

Most cultures, including our own, do not value the poor. They hold up the rich, the powerful, and the successful, no matter how their riches or power were obtained. The rich man in my story would be the valued one, while the first man in my story would be pushed to the margins of society and likely blamed for its ills. These poor are usually considered by the powerful in their society to be *poor souls*—people to be pitied. On the other hand, the kingdom of God values the poor. God values the poor so much, that God claims them as heirs of the kingdom. The kingdom also values those who are poor in spirit, if they recognize their spiritual poverty or their state of being *poor souls* and turn to God.

Wealth is more than a societal value. Too often it comes about because of a system that benefits the rich and keeps the poor in bonds of poverty. These structures are political, economic, and military, and are set in stone by banks, international business concerns, and governments. Frequently referred to as "structural poverty," it is precisely because of the near impossibility of changing these structures that Jesus gives special recognition to the poor. In Latin America, nearly all the established structures favor the rich man in the story above, while the same structures keep the poor man and his family in poverty.

BECOMING THE POOR IN SPIRIT

For most of my adult life, I have struggled with the differences between the two men I learned to know. I always evaluated myself with Luke's version of this beatitude. In Luke 18:22 Jesus told the rich young ruler to "sell everything you have and give to the poor." What does that mean for me personally? Among numerous things, it has led me to choose a simpler lifestyle, making choices not to accumulate or hoard material goods. I have never owned a new car and, for many years, eschewed owning property. To break the power of the structures, I have bought fair trade products, try to buy local foods, and limit my purchases at mega-department stores.

Even so, while looking at the ever upwardly spiraling lifestyles of my peers, and the downward slides of many of my friends in Latin America, I became cynical, irate, and resentful. I lashed out at capitalism and multi-national corporations for their structures and unjust policies which perpetually keep wealth in the hands of a few. Ironically, I did not recognize my own poverty of the soul. I had gradually, and unwittingly, become a *poor soul*—that *someone* to be pitied.

Fortunately, I found the solution to my own problem as close as the poor man in my story. The poor man recognized his dependence on God and his neighbors. He lived in gratitude, knowing that he did not belong to himself. He was the perfect description of Johannes Metz, who argued that "In poverty of spirit we learn to accept ourselves as beings who do not belong to ourselves."[17] "To be able to surrender oneself and become *poor* is, in biblical theology, to be with God; to find one's hidden nature in God; in short, it is *heaven*." [18]

Self-surrender, ego surrender, and self-abandonment are not easy in any culture and are certainly more difficult in our individualistic one. Nevertheless, the more I can learn to abandon my own wants and needs and surrender to God, the more I will be able to become poor in spirit.

This encounter with two strangers—both poor in spirit—taught me the lesson of letting go. Without it, I might have missed the exhilaration of being blessed and grateful and bound to God in deeper relationship.

MEDITATION AND GUIDED PRAYER

1. Meditation and prayers of disorientation

a. Spend a few moments in silent reflection. Think of a time when you have encountered a stranger who was economically poor, or was poor in spirit, or who was *to be pitied*. Think of your reactions to him or her. Were your reactions of pity? Contempt? Compassion?

b. Think of a time when you were *poor in spirit*, broken, and felt marginalized. How did you feel? How did other people react to you? Describe your disorientation.

c. Reflect on what structures, systems, people you have encountered that perpetuate the conditions of poverty you saw or that triggered your own feelings of being marginalized or broken.

d. Reflect on your ability or your group's ability to change the situation of poverty in which the stranger you met is caught.

e. Dear God, I do not understand why there is such a great divide between the haves and the have-nots in our world; between those who seem to have it all together and those who are broken. It makes me furious. Aren't you a God of justice? Why do you allow some to have so much and so many to have so little?

2. Meditation and prayers of confession and reorientation

a. Spend a few moments in silent reflection. Think of where you might have seen God at work despite the dire needs of the poor stranger or despite your own brokenness.

b. Think of times when you were able to let go and surrender to God.

c. Reflect on how you might respond, even in small symbolic ways, to the injustice and the poverty you encountered or to your own disorientation.

d. Reflect on how the poor stranger's story changed your perspective, your values, your life, even helping you to deal with your own suffering.

e. Dear God, I confess that your ways are bigger than my ways. Even though I do not understand why there is so much poverty and injustice in the world and so much brokenness, I have come to understand that you make yourself known amid such suffering. Therefore, I turn to you with gratitude because you have helped me to understand the blessing that is to be gained through surrender, commitment, and seeing your hand in everything. May your will be done in earth as it is in heaven. Amen.

BEATITUDE 2

Matt. 5:4: *Blessed are those who mourn, for they will be comforted.*

STORY

Davidcito died when he was about thirteen years old. His body was small and frail from lack of food and water, not because his parents weren't able to offer him enough food—he simply couldn't eat it. When he was around three, he swallowed a can of Draino, and the poison burned a permanent hole in his esophagus. A quick response with adequate medical help would have saved Davidcito, but this was not available in the family's rural Mexican town.

The feeding tube inserted through Davidcito's throat was a constant nuisance to him. Eating did not bring him pleasure since he could not taste and savor food in his mouth. He just didn't understand the need to eat and slowly died of starvation.

I was extremely apprehensive about going to the wake, since this was my first, and I wasn't familiar with all the social conventions of rural Mexico. However, I entered their home and sat with Davidcito's large extended family in a small, dark room which normally served as the family's living room. His smallish casket lay at the head of the room with lit candles flickering around it. The family planned to remain there all night before the burial the next day.

What I experienced that night took me aback. Instead of a somber, tearful vigil, what I noticed was more of a family reunion. People laughed and told stories about Davidcito and the rest of the family. Food and drink was freely passed around and enjoyed.

It was not that Davidcito's family wasn't sad. No one could argue how much he meant to them, as witnessed by the great lengths and expense they went to in seeking out many medical experts who could possibly save his fragile life. Their grief was deep, but most notably, the family of Davidcito was surrounded by family and friends in their time of mourning and were comforted by them.

REFLECTION

Two things emerged about this event for me after years of living in the culture. The first is that death in Mexican culture tends to be accepted as part of the ebb and flow of life. No one can escape it; it just comes sooner to some than to others. Secondly, when there is a need in the community, Mexicans flock together to hold each other up. For them, burdens are not meant to bear alone and in silence as people in my culture so often do. They support each other with their presence and are comforted.

True, those mourning Davidcito were sad. True, they wept mournful tears. Yet, they simply understood that being in each other's company was far more comforting than bearing the pain alone.

CONFLICTING CULTURAL VALUES

U.S. American culture and many individuals in all cultures look down on people who are dependent on others and can't *grin and bear it* alone. U.S. American culture and others value the strong, unemotional individualist who shows strength through cold perseverance in time of adversity. Our culture teaches to need no one; we do not want to be dependent on anyone. In addition, many cultures value a superficial happiness that glosses over unmet needs. The kingdom of God, on the other hand, values people who humbly share their hurts and pains openly with others and God. They are comforted and find a deep, soul-satisfying joy.

Becoming Those Who Mourn

When I look at the conditions of the world in which we live, I find many places to mourn. Nevertheless, the tendency is for me to become upset and cynical at the overwhelming injustice, racism, hate, and brokenness that is everywhere. Yet this anger and this cynicism really do nothing to make the world better. Instead, they make me resentful and bitter. Resentfulness and bitterness are not traits of the kingdom. In place of anger and bitterness, I need a calmness of spirit. In place of resentfulness, I need gratitude. To reach these kingdom values, like many people in all cultures who have experienced deep loss, I need to learn to mourn.

Henri Nouwen expresses it this way: "When I consider the immense waywardness of God's children, our lust, our greed, our violence, our anger our resentments, and when I look at them through the eyes of God's heart, I cannot but weep and cry out in grief."[19] Nouwen includes himself in his indictment of humankind with the pronoun *our*. I, too, cannot overlook the propensities of my own heart to these same traits that make me so annoyed and resentful. I have reason to mourn for both my personal waywardness as well as the waywardness of our world. The kingdom seems a long way off.

When I consider the brokenness of young people who enter my classrooms—many scarred for life from abuse, parental breakups, suicides of friends—I am brought to tears. How can human beings be so cruel to each other? My tears identify me as a mourner and help me to begin to relate to those who suffer in my midst. Nouwen states: "There is no compassion without many tears."[20]

Instead of *grinning and bearing* the situations that affect me and those that surround me, what if I pray with tears of grief and mourning? Instead of bottling up the anger and resentment, which make me a restless and bitter person, what if I let my tears flow in deep grief to take on the pain of the brokenness around me? Instead of *going it alone*, what if I surround myself with fellow mourners so we can lift each other up in our troubles? In learning how to mourn, I will be comforted.

Mourning strangers taught me the importance of this kingdom trait. This encounter deepened my relationship with God and helped me to be blessed as well as grateful.

MEDITATION AND GUIDED PRAYER

1.Meditation and prayers of disorientation
 a. Spend a few moments in silent reflection. Think of a time when you experienced a loss. How did you feel? Was it unfair? Remember a friend or a stranger who was mourning a loss. What was your response to him or her? Were your reactions of pity? Of compassion?
 b. Reflect on how other people responded to you about your loss. Was the response helpful or hurtful?
 c. Reflect on the amount of brokenness in our world and even in your own life—poverty and oppression, abuse and violence, hatred and racism. How does it make you feel?
 d. Dear God, there are times when I just don't understand your ways. When I have suffered loss, where were you? Whenever I think of how much pain there is in the world, I get upset, frustrated, and confused. Where are you in all of this? Don't you care about your creation? Why do you allow so much suffering to happen?

2.Meditation and prayers of confession and reorientation
 a. Spend a few moments in silent reflection. Think of when you might have felt God's presence during your dark-

est times of mourning your loss. Think of how your friend or a stranger dealt with their loss. Reflect on what brought them around.

b. Think of times when you were able to let your tears of mourning flow for your own losses, for the losses of friends or strangers, and for the brokenness of our world.

c. Reflect on where other people touched you deeply with their care and compassion during your disorientation. How did this "turn your mourning into dancing?"

d. Think about how you will change your life to incorporate what you've learned from your mourning or another's mourning.

e. Dear God, I confess that I don't always understand your ways. Yet I thank you for allowing me to let go of my tears and mourn my losses. Thank you for friends who held me close when I was amid the darkness of mourning. Thank you for allowing me to sense your presence even at the moment that you felt the farthest away. With gratitude I come to you. You have shown me how without mourning there can be no dancing. Without seeking the comfort of other people I cannot be comforted. Help me to continually strive to see your light behind the darkness of the moment. May your will be done on earth as it is in heaven. Amen.

BEATITUDE 3

Matt. 5:5: *Blessed are the meek for they will inherit the earth.*

STORY

Doña Josefina cooked for our small band of MCC volunteers, rebuilding homes after a powerful earthquake wiped out a large percentage of her small Guatemalan town. *"No soy nada"* (I am nothing), she kept repeating over and over again. Being a woman, she was near the bottom of the social ladder in her culture. Being a woman who couldn't bear children forced her even lower down the ladder. Then, to make matters worse, being a woman deserted by her husband because of barrenness landed her only a few rungs above prostitutes and other lowlifes.

She had been told so often that she was nothing. She internalized it and believed it to be true. She learned to be quiet, to bear her humble position patiently. When our MCC group asked her to cook for us, it elevated her status a bit, for which she was quite proud. The cruel reality on her mind, though, was that in three months we would leave the village, and she would go back to being a nothing—a nobody.

Reflection

Josefina did not volunteer to be meek and marginalized. She was pushed there by her circumstances. Every society has those whom it puts at the bottom and then walks all over until their spirits are crushed. If I read this beatitude correctly, women like Josefina will inherit the earth. They will be the important ones in God's economy. What position of honor she lacks today, she will more than make up for in God's kingdom.

What are the structures in your society that push people to the margins, making them seem nobodies? Institutional racism, sexism, ageism, to name a few, are part of the social fabric of each culture. Even in many church institutions, deference is given to those with higher degrees and titles. At the institution where I work, professors many years ago were called "brother and sister." Today they are often referred to as Doctor so-and-so, Professor or Dean so-and-so—ever widening the gap between the meek who clean the toilets and the elite at the top.

As disciples of Christ, it's important to ask hard questions about how we build institutions and where being meek fits into those structures. As individuals, how do we voluntarily become meek to inherit the kingdom? What are the traits of being meek? The Greek word used here is *praus* and means "wholly relying on God rather than [one's] own strength to defend [one's self] against injustice."[21] Webster's first meaning is similar: "bearing difficulties or injuries with patience and humility." What better example than Josefina!

Conflicting Cultural Values

Few cultures value meekness. Nor do many value patience and humility in the face of injustice. In fact, the most used synonym for meek is "submissive." Patience and humility are also relegated to submissiveness. To most of us, this means being a doormat, allowing everyone to run over us. Instead, our culture along with others values assertiveness, aggressiveness, and brazen defense of our own rights.

These individualistic behaviors are embedded in the systems and structures that cultures build and perpetuate the marginalization of others. In our culture and many others, the meek inherit the dung heap because they wholly rely on God rather than their own strength. In God's kingdom, on the other hand, meekness is valued—the meek inherit everything. To be meek means putting others before ourselves and patiently enduring whatever comes our way.

Becoming Meek

Being white and male, wherever I have traveled—especially in Latin America—I have experienced far more "white privilege" and male deference than injustice. I have usually been treated with utmost respect and taken places where only the privileged are allowed to go. Although I have been wronged at times by others like everyone else, I have not experienced much institutional injustice like the characters in my stories. Haughtiness has been easier to attain than meekness.

The resultant ego inflation makes me more demanding wherever I go. When I don't get my way I become disgruntled, resentful. My blood pressure rises. If not outwardly, inwardly I throw a tantrum. I actually think I'm experiencing injustice! But the irony is this: I am relying on my own sense of "privilege" as a white male and a U.S. American rather than being dependent on God.

Once again, ire and resentment dominate the character of the non-meek. Kerry Walters calls this egotistical reaction a "beast," noting that "a 'meek' person is the one who tames the savage beast within us."[22] Being able to tame this beast goes against every fiber of our human ego and socialized behavior. Cultivating humility and patience is just as difficult.

Only as we learn to be still and listen for the voice of God within us can we overcome the beast. Walters says it this way, "Listening is only possible when we become quiet—when our will ceases its noisy and self-important maneuvering, when we finally acknowledge defeat and lay down our arms."[23] Acknowledging defeat allows us an unlikely victory over our ego- and ethnocentric values.

It took an encounter with a meek and marginalized stranger for me to understand the need for meekness. Since the warring for self has quieted, and I'm learning the gift of dependence on God, the path of meekness has led into once hidden corners where blessing and gratitude wonderfully hint at the inheritance to come.

MEDITATION AND GUIDED PRAYER

1. Meditations and prayers of disorientation

    a. Spend a few moments in silent reflection. Think of a time when you have encountered a stranger who is meek, someone who was "bearing difficulties or injustice with patience and humility." Think of your reactions. Pity? Contempt? Compassion?

    b. Think of a time when you felt the meekest, the most humble. What caused this meekness? Describe your disorientation.

    c. Reflect on what structures, systems, people you have encountered that push other people (the stranger) or yourself to the margins and crush their/your spirits.

    d. Reflect on your ability or your group's ability to change the situation of meek strangers so they experience simple dignity. Or what could have changed your own situation of undeserved meekness?

    e. Dear God, I do not understand why some people are pushed to the margins and picked on until their spirits are crushed. I don't know why I've needed to feel such alienation either. Why do I have to feel like a nobody? It makes me upset. Aren't you a God of justice? Why do you allow some to live lives of privilege while others are pushed to the margins?

2. Meditation and prayers of confession and reorientation

    a. Spend a few moments in silent reflection. Think of where you have seen God at work despite the brokenness of the meek stranger or in your own situation of meek disorientation.

   b. Think of times you were not forced to become meek by circumstances but able to "tame the savage beast" of arrogance within you to become meek, humble.

   c. Reflect on how you might respond, even in small symbolic ways to the marginalized meek you encountered or to your own sense of estrangement. Or think of ways that you can change your life to incorporate meekness into your daily walk, if you do not already feel at the margins.

   d. Reflect on how the meek stranger's story made you realize how often you take your privilege for granted. How difficult it is to "bear your difficulties with patience and humility."

   e. Dear God, I confess that your ways are bigger than my ways. Even though I do not understand why some people's spirits are crushed to where they think they are a nobody, I have come to understand that you make yourself known amid such marginalization. Help me to affirm where you are working despite the overwhelming brokenness. Once again I turn to you in gratitude. You have helped me to understand the blessing that is to be gained through waiting patiently with humility. Help me to continually see your hand at work even when I am most down and out, alienated and abandoned. May your will be done in earth as it is in heaven. Amen.

BEATITUDE 4

Matt. 5:6: *Blessed are those who hunger and thirst after righteousness [justice] for they will be filled.*

STORY

Mercedes studied her Bible in rural El Salvador and came to the conclusion that she needed to improve the lot of her fellow villagers. Many of them could not read and write, so when they took their bags of cotton to the local landowner to sell them, even though he told them they had 100 pounds of cotton, he wrote down fifty, and they didn't know the difference. Mercedes decided she would do something about this injustice so, along with the local priest, she began simple literacy and arithmetic lessons.

Because her fellow villagers were brought out of their ignorance and could no longer be exploited by the wealthy, Mercedes was considered a threat to their privileged position. One day local officials captured her, tortured her mercilessly, and threw her on a pile of bodies—leaving her for dead. She was eight months pregnant and, incredibly, gave birth while lying injured on the heap of bodies. Someone passing by happened to hear the baby's cry and discovered that Mercedes was still miraculously alive, even though her newborn baby perished.

Mercedes now tells her story wherever she can and works valiantly to abolish torture, especially to abolish training centers (such as the one in Ft. Benning that the United States uses to train Latin American militaries). Despite threats to her life, she continues to work for justice.

Reflection

Mercedes hungered and thirsted after righteousness (justice!) in her community, in her land. The Greek word translated as righteousness in this verse is *dikaiosune*,[24] which is rendered *justice* in my Spanish and German Bibles. That gives the meaning of the verse a different slant from the English word *righteousness*, which has come to signal personal piety and virtue rather than justice. One cannot strive for justice without encountering structures which perpetuate oppression.

Unjust structures caused the war in El Salvador and other Central American nations during the 1970s and 1980s. The Cold War was in full swing, and there was an ideological battle between the West and the Soviet Union for the hearts and minds of Central Americans. Although the fight appeared, on the surface, to be ideological—a battle between communism and democracy—the underlying reason was to gain economic control of the natural resources in the region. Large multi-national corporations, mostly from the United States, working together with local oligarchies, controlled the majority of the land.

Those seeking justice in the region asked for more equitable distribution of the land to provide the oppressed not only with some dignity but also to allow them some control of their own destinies instead of working in virtual slavery for multi-national corporations. People like Mercedes, who dared to work for change in the unjust structures, were labeled Communist by those who wanted to retain control of the resources. This allowed local armies, financed and trained by the U.S. government, to oppress, torture, and kill those who challenged their established systems.

Mercedes fell into the grip of the structures and powers who were against change. Because her sin was hungering and thirsting for justice, the powers condemned her to torture and death.

What does it mean to hunger and to thirst? These are two of our most basic needs. We eat and drink and become satisfied for the moment, but we soon become hungry and thirsty again. Do we hunger and thirst for justice in the same way as hunger and thirst for food and drink? Are we always seeking something better for those suffering from injustice by speaking against structural oppression? Mercedes courageously did this for her village.

CONFLICTING CULTURAL VALUES

Most cultures value the person who strives for retributive justice—giving the offender what he/she deserves. We see this time and again when people try to get revenge toward an offender, either through the courts or through their own personal vendettas. The kingdom of God, on the other hand, values the person who strives for restorative justice—giving both the victim and the offender their dignity instead of giving them what they deserve, restoring the relationship between the two. People who struggle for this justice will find that their longings and hungers will be filled.

BECOMING ONE WHO HUNGERS AND THIRSTS AFTER JUSTICE

As expressed earlier in the other Beatitudes, I too often have been incensed by the injustice I have witnessed in Latin America. The term *righteous indignation*, which I have used to excuse myself, does not excuse the projection of my rage onto the rich perpetuators of injustice and passive Christians who sit with their hands tied in *righteous piety*. The rage morphs into resentfulness and hate. These are not kingdom values.

What if instead I channel that rage into hungering and thirsting after justice? Ronald Rolheiser, in his book *Holy Longing*, claims that seeking justice is a non-negotiable pillar of Christian spirituality, "to change the world in such a way that people are *willingly willing* to live in a way that makes justice possible requires an appeal to the heart that is so deep, so universal, and so moral that no person of good conscience can walk away from it."[25]

That appeal, for the Christian, can only be made if change is done in the same way as Jesus modeled it. Rolheiser says "the fuel that fires our quest for justice must be drawn from the same source as the truth of justice itself, namely, from the person and teaching of Jesus."[26] Jesus' teaching from Matthew 25 embodies the truth that "our standing with God depends upon how we stand in relationship to the weakest members within society [and the world]."[27]

So often my motivation for striving after social justice has been tainted with non-Jesus-like attitudes and practices. Rolheiser's list of these problematic attitudes[28] mirror most of my own and I paraphrase them below.

- I can be arrogant and ugly to those who oppose me because my cause is so worthwhile.
- My private life and morality have no bearing on my work toward social justice.
- Prayer for justice is unnecessary; I only need to work for it.
- I want immediate results—I don't have the patience to wait for God's timing.
- I may exaggerate the actual conditions of injustice to make a stronger case for my cause.

To be honest, the problem of injustice and the structures that perpetuate it are so large that no individual can accomplish much. It takes standing with others working together, whether it be the church or other solidarity groups. Rolheiser said it well: "The compass of postmodern spirituality points not to rampant individualism and its violent outcroppings but to the importance of community and tradition, prizing human solidarity and peace."[29]

Like the meek, I am learning to sit in patience and wait for God's voice—not my own. At the same time, like those hungering and thirsting after righteousness, I find strength in joining church and other solidarity groups who are working on just causes. Only by recognizing my own participation in unjust structures and my own propensity to dominate and abuse, can I turn my ire and resentment into joy and gratitude.

It took an encounter with a stranger who worked for justice at the cost of her own safety for me to comprehend hungering and thirsting for justice. This encounter brought me into the presence of a God who is constantly attuned to injustice and nourishes me with blessing and gratefulness.

MEDITATION AND GUIDED PRAYER

1. Meditations and prayers of disorientation

a. Spend a few moments in silent reflection. Reflect on the difference in English between the word *righteousness* and *justice*. Think of a time when you have encountered a stranger who was working for justice. Did you think they were doing Jesus' work or did you think they were too political or too radical?

b. Reflect on a time when you were denied justice or when you were the victim of injustice. How did you feel? Describe your disorientation.

c. Reflect on what structures, systems, people cause unjust conditions in the world. How do they make you feel?

d. Reflect on your ability or your group's ability to change the many situations of the injustice in our world that you have read about or experienced.

e. Dear God, I do not understand why there is such injustice in the world. I do not understand why so often people who work for justice are labeled radicals and are ostracized by well-meaning Christians. It makes me furious. Aren't you a God of justice? Don't you want all of your people to live in dignity?

2. *Meditation and prayers of confession and reorientation*

a. Spend a few moments in silent reflection. Think of where you might have seen God at work in situations of injustice, either through organizations or individual people like Mercedes. Think about the people who defended you when you experienced an unjust situation.

b. Reflect on how the story of the stranger in the story who worked for justice made you change your perspective on what to *hunger and thirst for righteousness* might mean for a Christian.

c. Think about people who *hunger and thirst after justice*. Think about what motivates them, how they garner resources to continue on despite enormous obstacles.

d. Reflect on how you might respond, even in small symbolic ways, to situations of injustice. Think of ways that you can change your life to incorporate what you have learned from the stranger who worked for justice in her village.

e. Dear God, I confess that your ways are bigger than my ways. Even though I do not understand why there is so much injustice in the world, I have come to understand that you make yourself known even amid the worst oppression and injustice. Now with gratitude I turn to you. You have helped me to understand the blessing that is to be gained by working for justice and right relationships—giving people the dignity they need. Help me to see your hand at work even in the worst situations of injustice, either done to others or to myself. May your will be done in earth as it is in heaven. Amen.

BEATITUDE 5

Matt. 5:7: *Blessed are the merciful, for they shall receive mercy.*

STORY

The lawyer representing the loan shark sat across the living room with a smug look on his face. He was not going to budge. Mennonite Central Committee had started building a home on the lot of Manuel when the loan shark declared that the property was no longer Manuel's, but his.

It all started when Manuel needed to borrow $1,000 for a medical emergency. Despite pooling money from all his family and friends, he could not come up with the full amount. As a last resort, Manuel turned to the loan shark and gave him the deed to his property—his only guarantee for the borrowed money.

Manuel had no concept of interest or guaranteeing his loan with the deed of his house. He needed the money immediately, and the going rate of ten percent per week of compound interest seemed under such circumstances a small price to pay. In his mind he only owed $1,000. He paid a little here and a little there, never realizing, until he wanted to build on his lot, that the interest had mushroomed into a huge debt of $10,000.

Now, two years later, the lawyer was here to collect. The lot which guaranteed his home was now being taken away. I used all the arguments and logic I could muster against the lawyer so that my friend could keep his lot. The more I argued, the more smug grew the lines around his mouth. He was not giving an inch.

Finally in desperation, I begged, "For the love of Jesus Christ and the Holy Catholic Church, have mercy on this poor man!" My plea fell on deaf ears. I walked away from the meeting a deeply disappointed and frustrated man.

Reflection

The poor man in the story did not receive mercy because all the economic structures in his small, rural town were set against him. He could not open a bank account because he didn't have enough money to deposit the minimum balance and leave it there. Had that been possible, when he needed a loan he could have turned to the bank, which was regulated by law, for borrowing money. Instead his only option was the loan shark. Having little capital and few material possessions, he had nothing except the deed to his land for collateral. The deed had been passed down from generation to generation.

Since he needed to work in the fields to help the family at an early age, Manuel had no schooling to help him understand the principle of interest. As a result, that one emergency wiped out everything he had. No one needed mercy more than he. Yet hundreds of people throughout the world, like Manual, are at the mercy of loan sharks and those who prey on the misfortunes of others.

In many ways developing countries are at the mercy of international banking structures in much the same way Manuel is at the mercy of the loan shark. Their national debts keep mushrooming, resulting in stagnating economies and hyperinflation. Pleas for debt reduction have fallen mostly on deaf ears. The wealthy get wealthier and the poor get poorer.

On a personal level, being merciful means giving someone unmerited favor, like when your friend throws a paper together an hour before class and gets an "A" on it, while you slaved in research for two weeks and only end up with a "B." Being merciful is rejoicing with the person who got the undeserved "A."

This goes completely against human nature. Yet this is what God has done for us. None of us deserves the love and the gift of his son. We have all received unmerited favor from God. Those who treat others like God has treated them will receive the same in return. I suspect that the unscrupulous men in my story, who have received more than their share on this earth will be surprised in the coming kingdom. I suspect that those who work to perpetuate unjust international economic systems will also be surprised. Because they were not merciful, they will receive no mercy.

Conflicting Cultural Values

Few cultures value being merciful. Our own culture values the cold, calculating executive who can make difficult decisions with little concern for how those decisions affect the lives of others. We hold up the Vanderbilts, the Roosevelts, the Gateses, and others who have amassed huge family fortunes without adequate concern for how the wealth was obtained. For most cultures, being merciful is a sign of weakness. The kingdom of God, on the other hand, values a merciful person—a person who knows how to forgive others for their shortcomings and how to rejoice with those who have received unmerited favor. Such a person will receive God's mercy and forgiveness.

Becoming the Merciful

There is no better image of mercy than the father in the story of the Prodigal Son (Luke 15:11-32). Even though the son wished him dead and squandered all his inheritance in lascivious and frivolous living, the father welcomed him home with loving and open arms. Instead of being punished or relegated to slave status he was completely restored to his position in the family as son and heir.

Mercy is not pity or feeling sorry for someone. "True [Christian] mercy must involve both an inner and an outer response"[30] claims Kerry Walters.

> Christian mercy . . . reaches far beyond the immediate emotion of sympathy. . . . Incalculably more important is its goal of breathing life into others, of enabling them to claim their identity and destiny as beings made in the likeness of God.[31]

Because of my cultural socialization, it has always been a struggle to be merciful—especially to those closest to me. Like meekness, being merciful seems to be something for the frail and the weak—not the strong male of my upbringing. However, like the mournful, I can recognize situations where mercy is needed and not only mourn the situation of need or injustice but respond accordingly.

My own journey has taken me to our local hospital as a volunteer chaplain for Latin American patients—many of whom are marginalized for a myriad of reasons. I have listened to countless stories of pain, both physical and institutional, and have responded with compassion and prayer, physically laying my hands on them. The act of listening and praying moves the encounter beyond pity into the realm of mercy.

In some small way, maybe I have been able to do what Walters suggests: "enabling [my patients] to claim their identity and destiny as beings made in the likeness of God."[32] I have been surprised on many occasions when recipients shed tears for my simple acts of service—tears of gratitude that someone from the dominant culture would take the time to listen to their story without condemnation and respond to their immediate need.

I have a long way to go to become merciful like the father in the story of the Prodigal Son. Nevertheless, experiencing a sense of God's presence with me and with the patients has filled my heart with gratitude.

It took an encounter with an unmerciful stranger for me to understand the need for mercy. This encounter helped me get a glimpse of God's mercy toward me, so that blessing and gratefulness are quick to rise up as mercy from me.

Meditation and Guided Prayer

1. Meditation and prayers of disorientation

a. Spend a few moments in silent reflection. Think of a time when you encountered a stranger who needed the mercy of someone in authority. Think of your reaction: Pity? Contempt? Compassion? How did you react to the man in the story who needed mercy?

b. Think of a time when you desperately needed someone's mercy. How did it make you feel? Describe your disorientation.

c. Reflect on what structures, systems, or people in the story perpetuate injustice without mercy or on what need for mercy occurred in your own life.

d. Reflect on your ability or your group's ability to change these unmerciful systems in which the stranger in the story is caught or the situations in which you are caught that necessitate mercy.

e. Dear God, I do not understand why people can act with such callousness in the face of such need. It makes me irate. Aren't you a God of justice? Aren't you on the side of those who need mercy? Why do you allow people to perpetuate such selfishness and arrogance in the face of such need?

2. Meditation and prayers of confession and reorientation

a. Spend some moments in silence. Reflect on how you might extend mercy to someone in need or where you have seen others extend such "unmerited favor" to others.

b. Think of when you yourself were extended mercy—unmerited favor. How did it make you feel?

c. Reflect on how the poor stranger's story changed your idea of mercy—your perspective, your values, your life—

and think of ways that you can change your life to incorporate extending more mercy to others.

d. Dear God, I confess that your ways are bigger than my ways. Even though I do not understand why you allow some people to take advantage of others without repercussions, I have come to understand that you make yourself known amid such cruelty. Thank you for people who are willing to be merciful to those who are in need of mercy, including myself. Now I turn to you in gratitude. You have helped me to understand the blessing that is to be gained through receiving and granting mercy. Help me to continually strive to be merciful as you are merciful. Help me to forgive and to accept forgiveness. May your will be done on earth as it is in heaven. Amen.

BEATITUDE 6

Matt. 5 8: *Blessed are the pure in heart, for they will see God.*

STORY

Latin machismo. I described the flirtatious, ogling behavior of my Latin American male friends to my U.S. Spanish class and my disgust came through. A Brazilian woman in the class took issue with my obviously U.S. American perspective and expressed a different view. "I would much rather have men comment about me to my face where I can deal with it, than to have filthy stuff written about me on locker room walls like you do here."

My students on intercultural study in Central America or Mexico often comment on how dirty everything is. People throw trash out of the windows of their cars—any time or place—and empty pop cans and candy wrappers are strewn all over the sidewalks, the inference being that U.S. Americans are so much more concerned about cleanliness.

When I compare what the Brazilian woman said about inner impurity with our culture's obsession with outer cleanliness, I hear Jesus' warnings to the scribes and Pharisees: "Woe to you, scribes and Pharisees, hypocrites! For you clean the outside of the cup and of the plate, but inside they are full of greed and self-indulgence" (Matt. 23: 25).

Reflection

Who are the pure in heart who will see God? These are people who are less interested in outward appearances and more interested in interior health. They understand their propensity for sin—anger, gluttony, lust, hate, murder, gossip, impatience, miserliness, and more. They are pure in heart because they, through meditation and prayer, have learned to walk in the light of Christ—how to transform the impure impulses of fallen creatures into life-giving action and pure living. Purity of heart is not a once-and-done thing, however. Prayer and meditation must continue because the propensity to sin is a persistent battle. Jesus railed against the smugness of those who thought they were holy and had progressed beyond the petty sins of the common people. Their holiness, while it may have looked admirable on the surface, did not stem from inner purity.

Conflicting Cultural Values

Most cultures, including our own, value outward appearance and conformity. People do not want to be seen as different or strange; we want to fit in. Most cultures have rote answers for greetings like "How are you?" because blurting out our true feelings seems rude. Most cultures have developed intricate ways of avoiding saying how they really feel, especially if it involves painful disclosure.

U.S American culture is particularly adept at hiding the parts of ourselves that seem unclean, even though they are part of what it means to be human. This hiding can result in sanctimoniousness rather than sanctification. In contrast, God's culture values the pure in heart—those who recognize their secret sins, expose them to Christ's light through prayer and public confession and become sanctified (pure).

BECOMING THE PURE IN HEART

Becoming pure in heart is no easy task! It means admitting my own inclination to sin. It means carefully confronting each flaw of the fallen human condition and admitting my inclination to be like that trait. The human tendency is to ignore the character flaw in myself or to project it onto other people who exhibit the same trait. The phenomenon of projection is a commonly understood psychological theory elaborated by Carl G. Jung but already identified by Jesus in his pithy statement in Matthew 7:3, "Why do you look at the speck of sawdust in someone else's eye and pay no attention to the plank in your own eye?"

I have always considered, at least intellectually, that racism is one of the lowest forms of human depravity. Many times people in Latin America would point out to me that their society was less racist than the U.S. American society, many claiming that no racism existed at all. Without challenging them, I made mental note of places in their language and actions where blatant racism was evident. By so doing, of course, I retained my smugness about racism.

To discover that I was racist was a shock! I was in the middle of preparing for a much-needed family vacation when my family and I were interrupted by a knock at the door. There on the doorstep was a family from one of the villages where Mennonite Central Committee (MCC) was building homes destroyed by an earthquake. Though they desperately wanted a home, after several meetings with them MCC determined that they did not meet the carefully laid out criteria for receiving a home.

Village lore also left us with the impression that on previous occasions this family had manipulated aid-givers into doling out services for which they were not entitled. This time they used their *Evangelical* card; that is, because they were Evangelicals they deserved a home more than their Catholic neighbors—something that went completely against MCC's policy in choosing who should or who should not receive a home.

The woman, toting a bare-bottomed toddler on her hip, as was the custom in her culture, tearfully pleaded her case despite our firm decision. To make matters worse, the child eliminated fecal matter all over the floor. The mother, pacing back and forth, noticed neither the stench nor the fact that she was smearing excrement all around our freshly mopped tile floor. I exploded—sent the family packing with sarcastic words and slammed the door.

I could not rest easily after that encounter. That day, the whole way to Guadalajara, our vacation destination, my thoughts returned to that family and my hateful reaction. Whenever I tried to sleep, the vision of their faces entered my consciousness. Of first concern was my anger, a character flaw so often projected on another person.

As I held the encounter up to the light of Christ, I discovered that my flaw went much deeper. Despite having lived in the Latin American culture nearly seven years, and despite learning all the *politically correct* responses to personal and institutional racism, when confronted with an actual situation, I was racist. True, this incident might have provoked disgust in most anyone—racist or not—and is not necessarily proof of my racist attitudes, but it triggered deeper reflection and awareness of attitudes hidden deep within myself.

Becoming aware of this sin was the first step. Praying carefully about turning my racist attitudes into love for all people was the next step which meant I needed to make it right with the family I had offended. Hard as it was, I went to them and asked for their forgiveness. They were astonished that a *patrón* would return and ask a *peón* for forgiveness. We made things right.

Racism is not only a personal sin but is woven into the very fabric of most societies. Institutional racism is rampant in Guatemala even though a peace agreement was signed in 1996, after nearly thirty years of war in which the Guatemalan army practiced genocide against the Mayan population who comprise the majority of the population. Institutional racism is still rampant in the United States despite major strides made in the civil rights movement and the election of Barack Obama. The church and its institutions too often have also been part of structural racism, whether in Guatemala or the U.S. or anywhere else in the world. Purity of structures is even more difficult to attain than purity of the individual heart. However, the alternative community Jesus inaugurated and that *sees God* cannot tolerate racism.

For every one of the individual sins listed above, there are examples of how I tend to ignore the log in my own eye and criticize the speck in the other's eye, just as I did with racism. I may not be totally free of racist attitudes, but I am *becoming* "pure in heart" by bringing into my consciousness and dealing with the racism I encountered within myself. As painful as the experience was, I can only feel gratitude for that one step forward on the way.

It took an encounter with several strangers for me to understand my propensity to project my own character flaws on others while excusing my own attitudes and behavior. This encounter stripped away the mask of smugness that I had been wearing and opened me to the purity of God's love for me and others, thus allowing a two-way flow of both blessing and gratitude.

MEDITATION AND GUIDED PRAYER

1. Meditation and prayers of disorientation

a. Spend a few moments in silent reflection. Think of a time when you had an extremely negative reaction to a stranger, someone different from you. Why did you react the way you did? Was something unacceptable about yourself festering deep within you?

b. Think of a time when you felt someone else projecting their character flaws on you. How did it make you feel? Describe your disorientation.

c. Reflect on what negative personality trait you were projecting on the stranger to whom you reacted so negatively. What *speck* you were seeing in his or her eye while avoiding the *plank* in your own?

d. Reflect on your ability to change this inner flaw on your own. Does it make you feel empowered or helpless?

e. Dear God, I do not understand why people project their own unresolved issues on to other people at certain times, often in anger. Why do I or others have such feelings if we are redeemed by you? Haven't you assured us of your presence? Why do you allow me to react in such an unchristian, even at times, inhuman manner?

2. *Meditation and prayers of confession and reorientation*

a. Spend a few moments in silent reflection. Think of where you might have seen God at work in your life despite your negative reactions to certain strangers and of times when you were able to let go of your resentment and love the stranger.

b. Reflect on how you might pray or sit in silence before God with your resentment. How might this change your feelings?

c. Think of ways you can change your life to incorporate what you have learned from your resentment of the stranger or how to continue showing mercy to those who have projected their unresolved issues on you.

d. Reflect on how your resentment of the stranger has transformed you and changed your perspective, your values, your life.

e. Dear God, I confess that your ways are bigger than my ways. Even though I do not understand why I get so resentful at certain people, I have come to understand that you make yourself known even amid such intense feelings. Thank you for showing me the *plank* in my eye through Jesus. Now I turn to you with gratitude. You have helped me to understand the blessing that is to be gained through understanding the difference between appearances and authentic being.

Help me ever strive for purity of heart in all situations. Help me to identify other areas of my life that need transformation. May your will be done in earth as in heaven. Amen.

❖ ❖ ❖

BEATITUDE 7

Matt. 5:9: *Blessed are the peacemakers, for they will be called the children of God.*

STORY

A friend of mine worked with Mennonite Central Committee during the height of the Sandinista-Contra war in Nicaragua in the 1980s. Because of his training and skills he was sent on a mission to bring peace between the Miskito Native peoples and the Sandinista regime.

For thirty-six years, a tyrannical government of three succeeding Somoza family members, propped up by the U.S., had virtually abandoned the Miskito peoples. They lived in the most isolated northeast corner of Nicaragua and enjoyed a way of life quite different from the Spanish/Mestizo culture that shaped most of the Nicaraguan people and their governments. In fact, the Miskito peoples historically had received little attention from any regime installed in Managua, the capital of Nicaragua.

Now that the left-leaning Sandinista regime was in power, the United States tried to exploit the tensions between Managua and the Miskito people as proof that the Sandinista government was illegitimate. Why there was no hue and cry from the U.S. government about this abandonment by their puppet and previous regimes makes their motives for the coming agitation quite clear.

Because the Sandinistas were unfriendly to U.S. business interests in Nicaragua, the U.S., at all costs, tried to undermine the legitimacy of the Sandinistas. One way of doing that was to exploit the cultural differences and tensions between the two groups. For example, the Miskito people are Moravian Evangelicals, and most of the people who have controlled the government in Managua, including the Sandinistas, were Catholic.

Through my friend's peacemaking efforts, the two Nicaraguan groups began to understand the cultural differences between them. As the two sides started coming together harmoniously through my friend's work, the U.S. government suddenly felt threatened. A plot was uncovered, revealing that the CIA, to maintain the controlling interests of the U.S. government in Nicaragua, planned to kidnap my friend's daughter and place a $10,000 price on her head—all because he heeded the call of Jesus in the Beatitudes to be a peacemaker.

Reflection

Being a peacemaker is as unnatural to most of our human socialization as fasting. Like dogs, we are programmed to defend our territory at all costs. After we have defended our immediate territory we set out to expand that territory by bringing more under our control. Dominating someone else for our own territorial expansion always builds up walls of hostility. The walls can be between individuals, tribes, or nations—walls producing generational anger which lashes out from time to time against whomever is feeling oppressed on the one side or threatened on the other.

To break down those dividing walls, which are sometimes centuries old, takes a special person. To be such a person, we must deal with our inner rage and propensity to lash out at the enemy. We need to be willing to sacrifice our own security to break down the walls of hostility. It cannot be done alone, without the help of God and the support of other like-minded individuals. Such people are the children of God.

Conflicting Cultural Values

Most cultures value violence. Most cultures' heroes and superheroes use might to make right. Doing anything else is for cowards and the weak. Most cultures set up systems, whether governmental or economic, which are kept in power by the force of armaments.

As territorial claims broaden, again whether governmental or economic, harsher means of enforcing the systems are put in place. In the 1970s and 1980s nearly every country in Latin America was ruled by a dictatorship, most of them put into power by U.S. intervention or persuasion. These brutal dictatorships were kept in power by the continual threat of terror. That era was riddled with disappearances, torture, and death by death squads. These régimes were legitimized by the U.S. government to protect their territorial economic grip on the region. In fact, many of the terror tactics used by the military and police forces in Latin America were trained in the School of the Americas (now called Western Hemisphere Institute for Security Cooperation) at Fort Benning, Georgia.

Peacemakers are seen as a threat when they try to settle differences through creative, unifying methods instead of the age-old violent, dividing ways. The kingdom of God values peacemakers—people who are able to reconcile warring factions with their enemies, people who are able to understand and control their wrath toward those who do wrong against them.

BECOMING A PEACEMAKER

Peacemaking is the result of taking the Beatitudes seriously and living them. Peacemaking contains all the elements of the Christian faith. It involves right relationships. Right relationships with God, with God's people, and with God's creation. It involves love. Proper love of self, love of God and creation, and love of all people—even our enemies. It is not passive, it is active; it is peace*making*, not peace*keeping*. Above all, it is following the way of Jesus, which was the way of the cross, where his power was "made perfect in weakness" (2 Cor. 12:9).

I have probably been more of a pacifier than a peacemaker, avoiding conflict wherever possible, *keeping my peace* and swallowing my consternation when wronged. Despite being socialized in a *peace* tradition of the Christian church, I have struggled to put my beliefs into action. I have worked diligently, if inconsistently, for a right relationship with God, as outlined in the other Beatitudes. I have worked hard at having right relationships with those I come into contact with on a daily basis, whether in the church or at work.

I have also volunteered in Latin America as a conscientious objector. This has included proclaiming my conviction that peace is better than war and that working to provide needed services to marginalized people is a more Christ-like way to bring understanding among the world's peoples than dropping bombs on them.

However, when it comes to peace at a larger level—a peace that includes justice—I come up short. My heightened sensitivity and strict judgment of myself in this area comes from direct involvement with people who desperately need peace with justice and frustration with how large the problem of bringing peace with justice really is. Like hungering and thirsting for justice, I cannot solve the world's problems alone. I need to do it in solidarity with the church, other Christians, and other groups working for God's will to be done *on earth as it is in heaven*.

It took an encounter with a friend who worked with strangers, trying to bring them together to avoid the violence of war, for me to understand the concept of peacemaking. This encounter helped me understand how God values the peacemaker's making of a place for both blessing and gratitude to flourish.

MEDITATION AND GUIDED PRAYER

1. Meditation and prayers of disorientation
   a. Spend a few moments in silent reflection. Think of a time when you encountered strangers or friends who were fighting each other. Think of your reactions to them. Were your reactions pity? Contempt? Compassion?
   b. Reflect on what kept these friends or strangers locked in enmity with each other. Family systems? Religious, political, or racial differences?
   c. Reflect on your own *enemies* or your struggles with honest confrontation with someone with whom you disagree. Does the situation seem hopeless?
   d. Reflect on your own or your group's ability to enable peacemaking between warring factions. Consider conflict between nations that has festered for years. How do these situations make you feel? Reflect on your own unresolved conflicts. Are you powerless before them?
   e. Dear God, I do not understand why there has to be so much enmity between people and nations. It seems there are always wars and hatred. I also do not understand why I cannot deal face-to-face with my conflicts. Both of these situations frustrate me until I become deeply disgruntled. Aren't you a God of peace? Why do you allow so much war and interpersonal conflict?

2. Meditation and prayers confession and reorientation
   a. Spend a few moments in silent reflection. Think of where you might have seen God at work through people working at peacemaking, like my friend in the story.
   b. Reflect on how you might learn to be a peacemaker or how you might deal better with personal conflict.
   c. Reflect on how my friend's story, the threats on his life and family, changed your perspective, your values, your life.

d. Think of ways that you can change your life to incorporate what you have learned about peacemaking from my friend.

e. Dear God, I confess that your ways are bigger than my ways. Even though I do not understand why there is so much war and hatred in the world, I have come to understand that you make yourself known amid such enmity. Thank you for those who are willing to work at peacemaking. I now turn to you in gratitude. Help me to continually strive, through Christ, to bring together people who are in conflict and to face my own disagreements and conflicts head on. May your will be done on earth as it is in heaven. Amen.

BEATITUDE 8

Matt. 5:10: *Blessed are those who are persecuted for righteousness' sake, for theirs is the kingdom of heaven.*

STORY

Carmen became an Evangelical Mennonite and attended the same church I did in La Ceiba, Honduras. Evangelical Mennonites lived out a new belief system and were often misunderstood by the general population. Carmen, one of the few young Evangelicals in our town, was harassed at every turn—going to school, going to the store, going to any friend's house—for what she believed. Her family even disowned her, and she was forced to live with an aunt.

Like many of those first Evangelicals in this town, she wanted an activity held at church every evening to help her remain strong in the face of verbal persecution. We had women's meetings Monday night, men's meetings Tuesday night, prayer meeting Wednesday night, Bible study Thursday night, youth group Saturday night, and both a morning and evening service on Sunday. By being with other Evangelical believers, Carmen's faith was strengthened, and she felt supported to continue her walk.

REFLECTION

How interesting that Jesus gives those who are persecuted the same blessing as the poor. The reason is because those who are persecuted are, like the poor and the meek, on the margins of their society. They are the people who get picked on because they are different. Who of us has been outwardly persecuted for our faith, let alone for *righteousness'* sake? Tertullian, an early church father, has said, "The blood of the martyrs is the seed of the church." Perhaps Jesus anticipated the coming persecution when he gave this beatitude, or perhaps he knew that the discipline of persecution purifies the church.

I would never glorify persecution or martyrdom, but there have been many instances throughout history of persecution bringing unprecedented growth to the church; the Mennonite church in Ethiopia being one recent example. Because of their marginalization, the persecuted become more dependent on God and on their community of faith.

In the U.S., most Christians are not marginalized. We are so assimilated into our individualistic, independent culture that unless we have a particular crisis, we live as if we have little need for God.

CONFLICTING CULTURAL VALUES

Most cultures pick on marginalized people because they are different. They don't conform to their society's standards, often because of their race, their religion, or their handicap. The racial profiling that is institutionalized in many countries is also a form of persecution.

Standing up for those who are mistreated by racial profiling is working for righteousness (justice!) and often leads to persecution—as does defending anyone at the margins. The kingdom of God values those who are at the edges of society—those who can't conform because of their race or religion or those who choose not to conform to their culture's norm.

Becoming the
Persecuted for Righteousness' Sake

I believe that if we take the Beatitudes seriously and live them, persecution follows in one way or another. The Beatitudes are so counter-cultural, and so against the structures and norms of most societies, that people who follow them are pushed to the margins and criticized, mocked and scorned, or much worse—in short, persecuted.

The closest I ever came to this was while working as a conscientious objector in Honduras as an alternative to military service during the Vietnam War. My job took me to a number of tourist regions, where I met many of U.S. American expatriates. Most of them admired me when I explained why I was in Honduras and what I was doing.

One individual, however, kept contradicting everything I said. He even went so far as to make fun of the work in which I was involved—work that had little to do with my pacifist stance except that it provided a means to fulfill my obligation to the U.S. government. He wasn't really nasty, but he definitely thought me a coward and had little regard for my desire to "build up rather than to destroy." I later discovered that the man had lost a son in the war and projected his frustration on me—a healthy, relatively safe CO who didn't need to face daily the possibility of death.

This experience was truly humbling. I reflected deeply on my motivations for registering as a CO. Did I really believe in my Christian stance, or was I trying to escape the horror of war? Was I just a Mennonite socialized by my peace tradition, acting on *the thing to do*? Maybe I actually was a coward. From then on, I never shared in cavalier style my faith or my service. Only deep personal convictions were acceptable reasons for registering as a CO, and it was critical to live out those convictions—with God's help—as best I could. To this day, those reflections mold how I live.

It took an encounter with a stranger for me to understand what it is like to be persecuted for righteousness' sake. This encounter helped me clarify my reasons for seeking a deeper relationship with God and to experience the blessing and gratitude that comes through that relationship even amid persecution.

MEDITATION AND GUIDED PRAYER

1. Meditation and prayers of disorientation

a. Spend a few moments in silent reflection. Think of a time when you have encountered or read about strangers persecuted for their faith. How did you react to them? With pity? Contempt? Compassion? Admiration?

b. Have you ever felt persecuted or tormented for your beliefs? How did it make you feel? Describe your disorientation.

c. Reflect on the religious and/or political structures or systems that caused this persecution either of others or yourself. Think about the many wars that have been fought over religious beliefs.

d. Reflect on your ability or your group's ability to change the structures that cause religious wars and persecution for a stranger's faith. Describe your feelings of hopelessness and frustration.

e. Dear God, I do not understand why there are so many different understandings of you that are divided up into different beliefs and faiths. It seems there are always wars and discrimination related to religious issues. It makes me mad. Shouldn't belief in you bring us together?

2. Meditation and prayers of confession and reorientation

a. Spend a few moments in silent reflection. Reflect on how you or other people have defended those who were being picked on for whatever reason: religion, race, gender, sexual orientation.

b. Think of times when you were able to defend someone who was being picked on. What helped you accomplish your task?

c. Reflect on how truly living the Beatitudes could cause you persecution from the larger culture—whatever culture that happens to be. Would that change your beliefs, your values, your life?

d. Think of ways that you can change your life to incorporate defending strangers'—often the marginalized of society—dignity.

e. Dear God, I confess that your ways are bigger than my ways. Even though I do not understand why there is so much religious enmity, I have come to understand that you make yourself known amid such enmity. I turn to you in gratitude. You have helped me to understand that working for the dignity of others and following your Beatitude ways may cause persecution. Yet the blessing for those of us who are picked on is nothing less than the kingdom of God! May your will be done in earth as it is in heaven. Amen.

BEATITUDE 9

Matt. 5:11: *Blessed are you when people revile you and persecute you and utter all kinds of evil against you falsely on my account. Rejoice and be glad for your reward is great in heaven, for in the same way they persecuted me and the prophets.*

STORY

While in Mexico with a church agency doing development work, one of my employees, whom I will call Nacho for the purposes of this story, did whatever he could to subvert my work and my person. He resented me because I was a U.S. American, because I was an Evangelical Christian, and because I controlled resources for reconstruction work in an earthquake-devastated town. My policy was to always treat my employees, whether Mexican or U.S. American, Evangelical or Catholic, with utmost respect. I assumed that openly sharing my feelings—both joy and frustration—would convey our common human connection.

One day I shared with this perceived rival my story of coming to Mexico, including details about all the doubts and shut doors for other opportunities. He totally misconstrued my openness and told everybody that I didn't want to be in Mexico. "He's just using the three years in Mexico as a stepping-stone, so he can climb to a higher administrative position in the agency." I never felt so betrayed in all my life! From then on, I didn't know what to share or what to withhold. Any move could be twisted to make me look bad.

Reflection

Being hated and accused falsely by someone is painful. People who hate and accuse others falsely are often projecting their own unresolved emotions onto the person being accused. Nacho was projecting his frustration with U.S. Americans and Evangelicals in general onto me because I represented those groups, even though I personally hadn't done anything to make him feel that way. Whatever I would have done would have irritated him.

People who live at the margin of society often receive similar projections from the majority culture. In fact, as we have seen so often in this study, societies build structures which reinforce this marginalization. Whether they are the poor, the handicapped, or of a particular ethnic, racial, or religious group, these people often feel the projection of being falsely accused. Once again, Jesus identifies with the people who are marginalized and falsely accused by society. Their reward will be great in heaven.

Conflicting Cultural Values

Most cultures find groups or individuals on which to project their own unresolved emotions—usually anger and hatred. Most cultures also find ways to institutionalize their projections, so that their projections seem natural and justified. They expect the *others*—the marginalized—to nicely conform to what has been defined as normal by the majority.

When they do not, the majority members, with their own unresolved frustrations, lash out with disdain and wrath against the downtrodden in hopes of feeling better about themselves. On the other hand, the kingdom of God values the misplaced and hated people. It saves for them the biggest reward in heaven.

BECOMING THE PERSECUTED

As a U.S. American, I was normally treated with special privilege wherever I traveled in Latin America. Most of the time, I could socialize with people of higher social standing than I could in my home country—feeling like a part of the upper crust. So the time I was "reviled" caught me up short.

It happened in 1969 when there was an escalation of conflict between Honduras and its neighboring country, El Salvador. This led to an El Salvadoran incursion into Honduran territory and the Honduran air force taking out the air force of El Salvador. Each side thought they were going to prevail until the Organization of American States (OAS) settled the conflict through negotiations. Both countries viewed the OAS as an instrument of the U.S. government and were critical of more U.S. intervention in the region.

After the settlement, I was asked to distribute material aid in the war-ravaged region of Honduras. On my way, I passed through San Pedro Sula, the largest city in Honduras. While walking down the street, a man cursed me, spit at me, and made it clear that my nationality was the cause of his hatred. I was taken aback! I had never been treated in this manner before—and haven't been since.

In this story, I was not reviled for the sake of Christ. I was reviled for being a U.S. American. I experienced this once. What must it be like to be reviled all the time for one's nationality, as so often happens in our world?

As mentioned earlier, I am convinced that if Christians took the Beatitudes seriously, and lived them, we would be persecuted or reviled by the prevailing culture simply because the Beatitudes are so counter-cultural—so against the norm—in nearly any culture.

It took encounters with various strangers for me to see how being reviled and being spoken falsely against can make a person feel. This encounter helped me find places where Christ dwells and to enjoy blessing and gratitude of kingdom hospitality.

Meditation and Guided Prayer

1. Meditation and prayers of disorientation

 a. Spend a few moments in silent reflection. Think of a time when you have been accused falsely, even if it wasn't for your faith. How did it make you feel? Have you ever been involved in hearing friends falsely accuse other friends? How did that make you feel?

 b. Reflect on what caused these times of being accused falsely. Was it jealousy? Your political or religious views? Your ethnic background or nationality?

 c. Think about the structures or worldview that caused the accuser to spread false stories about you or your friends. Describe your feelings of hopelessness and frustration in trying to help that person see things from your or your friend's perspective.

 d. Dear God, I do not understand why you allow people to accuse each other falsely, for whatever the reason. Why do you allow others to spread gossip and lies about me and my friends? It really perturbs me. Shouldn't Christians especially be above such behavior?

2. Meditation and prayers of confession and reorientation

 a. Spend a few moments in silent reflection. Think of times when you or your friends were able to bring together people who had falsely accused each other. What helped you bring this about?

 b. Reflect on how you might be reviled and mocked because of your faith or because of defending others' dignity.

 c. Reflect on how truly living the Beatitudes could cause a larger culture, no matter which one, falsely to accuse you. Would that change your beliefs, your values, your life?

 d. Think of ways that you can change your life to incorporate defending strangers'—often the marginalized of society—dignity in the face of many false accusations.

e. Dear God, I confess that your ways are bigger than my ways. Even though I do not understand why people continue to gossip and spread lies about each other, I have come to understand that you have been present on many occasions to repair the relationships that were hurt because of the false accusations. In gratitude, I turn to you because you have helped me to understand that by working for the dignity of others, and by following your ways from the Beatitudes, I myself may be falsely accused and reviled. Thanks for your blessing me with a reward in heaven. May your will be done in earth as it is in heaven. Amen.

BEATITUDE 10

Paraphrased, invented beatitude from Matt. 19:30 and 20:16 and what seems to be a theme of the book of Matthew: *Blessed are the last for they will be first in the kingdom of heaven, and woe to the first for they will be last.*

STORY
The young leaders of the Mennonite church in Mexico loved to tell the story of a former missionary among them. Several times a month, the church held a game night when the missionary and all the pastors and church leaders in Mexico City came together to fellowship in a non-church kind of way. After several months of playing together, the young leaders noticed that the missionary never won; in fact, it seemed that he deliberately played the games to lose. In their fierce competitiveness, they had failed to realize what was happening until months had passed. They had no idea how eager they were to use any means to win—how competitive they were. The quiet non-competitiveness of the missionary left a deep impression on them.

Reflection

The last will be first and the first last. What does this mean? As we look through the Beatitudes and the strangers whom we've met in this study, it seems clear who is last: the man who had the simple Mennonite Central Committee dwelling; the families of Davidcito, Josefina, Mercedes; the indebted man; the peacemaker; Carmen; and the missionary.

These people either had little in the world's eyes or had given up what they had to work for the kingdom. These people had little value in the larger scope of things. Society looked down on and in many cases trampled on them. They had little worth except to provide the rich and the powerful with more cheap labor. They all could have repeated, in the words of Josefina, "*No soy nada.*" (I am nothing.) Yet, as we have seen, these people are valuable in the kingdom of heaven. In fact they are blessed! Not only blessed, but heirs to quite a few promises!

- Theirs is the kingdom of heaven (vv. 3,10)
- They will be comforted (v. 4)
- They will inherit the earth (v. 5)
- They will be filled (v. 6)
- They will receive mercy (v. 7)
- They will see God (v. 8)
- They will be called children of God (v. 9).

Conflicting Cultural Values

Our businesses and other enterprises are structured so that the people with seniority and more education are typically rewarded with higher salaries. They are the first, at the top of the ladder. I have often wondered why Christian institutions operate on the same principles as secular institutions rather than the models Jesus has given us in the Beatitudes.

Often those who enter our places of employment are recent college graduates, young and indebted. Many are buying homes for the first time and starting families. Their financial needs are probably greater than at any other time in their life. Yet, because of the salary scales, their pay is the lowest.

They are the last, at the bottom of the ladder. Many employees who are nearing retirement, on the other hand, have their homes paid for and their children are independent. Their financial needs are fewer. Yet because of seniority, and sometimes education, they are paid the highest salaries.

What if Christian institutions came up with some creative models to address this *first/last* situation? What if Christian institutions creatively looked at the disparity between the pay received by the CEO at the top and the janitor at the bottom of the pay scale as well? These are challenges we face when we take the Beatitudes seriously.

On the competitive, individualistic level, most cultures do not value losers—people who come in last. We try any means to be first. It matters little whether we are on a sports field, in an artistic endeavor, or in a corporate boardroom, being number one is the primary motivator in our individualistic, capitalistic culture. Playing a game deliberately to lose, like the missionary in the above story, is inconceivable in our reality. More common is the use of unscrupulous means to leap over others to get to the top.

When someone wins, however, someone else has to lose. Perhaps instead of winning or losing, we could strive, rather, for mutual respect. Nevertheless, Jesus makes it clear that those who are first now will be last in the kingdom of heaven; and that those who are now last, at the bottom of the heap, on the lowest rung, will be first.

BECOMING THE LAST INSTEAD OF THE FIRST

After I returned from a stint with Mennonite Central Committee in Mexico, I wanted to find a way, at least symbolically, to lower my ego demands for always being first. I also wanted to honor the politeness that Mexican culture afforded me at every opportunity. By performing this symbolic act, I would remind myself that I was not better than anyone else and, in a way, become last instead of first.

At the time, I worked at Hesston College a small, two-year college in central Kansas, which had a number of international students. The building where my office was located had several classrooms, so many people—faculty, staff, and students—came in and out its doors. My symbolic act was that I would never enter a door ahead of someone else.

For the most part, this did not seem to bother U.S. Americans, no matter what age, but it became a real dilemma for Japanese students. They had been taught to give deference to older people and people with higher stations in life. For their culture, I fit both criteria. So when we approached the same door, they would signal for me to go in, but I would insist that they go first. Sometimes it took quite a while for those students, who normally considered themselves *lower*, to allow themselves to enter before the *higher* person.

This little exercise constantly reminded me of my experiences in Latin America. It helped me be meek and humble and to remember that the first will be last and the last will be first in God's kingdom.

It took an encounter with strangers who experienced a rather unsettling encounter with a missionary for me to understand the idea of not always placing myself first. This encounter helped me value the way in which Christ lowered himself to dwell among us as a stranger and enabled me to see the blessing and gratitude in doing the same for others.

MEDITATION AND GUIDED PRAYER

1. Meditations and prayers of disorientation

a. Spend a few moments in silent reflection. Think of a stranger who you view as being at the *bottom of the heap*, the *lowest* on your social stratification. Why are they at the bottom? How do you react to them? With pity? Contempt? Compassion?

b. Think of a time when you were last and thought you should be higher—either in a game or some other social endeavor. How did being last make you feel?

c. Reflect on what structures, systems, people you have encountered that place people at the bottom of their society's totem pole or something which caused you to be *last*.

d. Reflect on your ability or your group's ability to change society or structures that marginalize certain people and place them at the bottom. Reflect on your ability to change the rules of the game or your ability to play the game that you continually lose. How does it make you feel?

e. Dear God, I do not understand why some people are at the top of social ladders and others are at the bottom. Why certain people are always winners while others are always losers. It isn't fair. It makes me irate, because often there are so few winners and so many losers. Aren't you a God of justice? Why do you allow some to have so much advantage and privilege while so many to have next to nothing?

2. Meditation and prayers of orientation

a. Spend a few moments in silent reflection. Think of times when you or someone you know were able to give up your own places of privilege to give a stranger dignity. Think of a time when you were given a higher place than society thought you deserved.

b. Reflect on how you might respond, even in small symbolic ways, to put others' needs ahead of your own or to forgive those who pushed you to the bottom.

c. Reflect on how the story of the missionary's deliberate denial of competitiveness challenged you or changed your perspective or your values.

d. Think of ways you can change your life to incorporate what you have learned from the non-competitive missionary.

e. Dear God, I confess that your ways are bigger than my ways. Even though I do not understand why certain people are marginalized and placed at the bottom of our social structures, I thank you for faithful servants who are willing to work with "the least of these" to lift them and give them dignity. With this same gratitude I turn to you. Help me to continually strive to see your hand at work even in uneven social ladders, and help me put your ways first. May your will be done on earth as it is in heaven. Amen.

Notes

1. David I. Smith, *Learning From the Stranger* (Grand Rapids: Eerdmans, 2009).
2. StudyLight.org, "Lexicons: Old Testament Hebrew, Old Testament and New Testament Greek" (Gdansk, Poland: StudyLight.org, 2001), http://www.studylight.org/lex/.
3. Douglas R. A. Hare, *Matthew: Interpretation, a Bible Commentary for Teaching and Preaching* (Louisville: John Knox Press, 1993).
4. William Barclay, *The Gospel of Matthew, The Daily Study Bible Series*, rev. ed., 2 vols. (Philadelphia: Westminster Press, 1975).
5. StudyLight.org, "Lexicons: Old Testament Hebrew, Old Testament and New Testament Greek."
6. Barclay, *The Gospel of Matthew*.
7. Hare, *Matthew*.
8. Hare, *Matthew*.
9. Provident Baptist Ministries, "The Beatitudes," *The Beatitudes* (2006), November 22, 2007, http://www.pbministries.org/books/pink/Beatitudes/beatitudes.htm.
10. J. Andrew Overman, *Matthew's Gospel and Formative Judaism: The Social World of the Matthean Community* (Minneapolis: Fortress Press, 1990).
11. Overman, *Matthew's Gospel and Formative Judaism*.
12. Mark Allan Powell, *God with Us: A Pastoral Theology of Matthew's Gospel* (Minneapolis: Fortress Press, 1995).
13. Barclay, *The Gospel of Matthew*.
14. Powell, *God with Us*.

15. Powell, *God with Us.*
16. Donald B. Kraybill, *The Upside-Down Kingdom*, A Christian Peace Shelf Selection, rev. ed. (Scottdale, Pa.: Herald Press, 1990).
17. Johannes Baptist Metz, *Poverty of Spirit*, rev. ed. (New York: Paulist Press, 1998).
18. Metz, *Poverty of Spirit.*
19. Henri J. M. Nouwen, *The Return of the Prodigal Son: A Story of Homecoming* (New York: Continuum, 1995).
20. Nouwen, *The Return of the Prodigal Son.*
21. StudyLight.org, "Lexicons: Old Testament Hebrew, Old Testament and New Testament Greek."
22. Kerry S. Walters, *Merciful Meekness: Becoming a Spiritually Integrated Person* (Mahwah, N.J.: Paulist Press, 2004).
23. Walters, *Merciful Meekness.*
24. StudyLight.org, "Lexicons: Old Testament Hebrew, Old Testament and New Testament Greek."
25. Ronald Rolheiser, *The Holy Longing: The Search for a Christian Spirituality*, 1st ed. (New York: Doubleday, 1999).
26. Rolheiser, *The Holy Longing.*
27. Rolheiser, *The Holy Longing.*
28. Rolheiser, *The Holy Longing.*
29. Rolheiser, *The Holy Longing.*
30. Walters, *Merciful Meekness.*
31. Walters, *Merciful Meekness.*
32. Walters, *Merciful Meekness.*

Works Cited

Barclay, William. *The Gospel of Matthew*. The Daily Study Bible Series. Rev. ed. 2 vols. Philadelphia: Westminster Press, 1975.

Hare, Douglas R. A. *Matthew: Interpretation, a Bible Commentary for Teaching and Preaching*. Louisville: John Knox Press, 1993.

Kraybill, Donald B. *The Upside-Down Kingdom*. A Christian Peace Shelf Selection. Rev. ed. Scottdale, Pa.: Herald Press, 1990.

Metz, Johannes Baptist. *Poverty of Spirit*. Rev. ed. New York: Paulist Press, 1998.

Ministries, Provident Baptist "The Beatitudes." *The Beatitudes*.August 13, 2006 (2006). November 22, 2007, http://www.pbministries.org/books/pink/Beatitudes/Beatitudes.htm

Nouwen, Henri J. M. *The Return of the Prodigal Son : A Story of Homecoming*. New York: Continuum, 1995.

Overman, J. Andrew. *Matthew's Gospel and Formative Judaism: The Social World of the Matthean Community.* Minneapolis: Fortress Press, 1990.

Powell, Mark Allan. *God with Us: A Pastoral Theology of Matthew's Gospel.* Minneapolis: Fortress Press, 1995.

Rolheiser, Ronald. *The Holy Longing: The Search for a Christian Spirituality.*first ed. New York: Doubleday, 1999.

Ryken, Leland, et al. *Dictionary of Biblical Imagery.* Downers Grove, Ill.: InterVarsity Press, 1998.

StudyLight.org. "Lexicons: Old Testament Hebrew, Old Testament and New Testament Greek." Gdansk, Poland, 2001. Web. Copyright © 2001-2007, StudyLight.org. http//:www.studylight.org/lex/. Accessed Nov. 22, 2007

Walters, Kerry S. *Merciful Meekness: Becoming a Spiritually Integrated Person.* Mahwah, N.J.: Paulist Press, 2004.

THE AUTHOR

Don Clymer was born in Lancaster, Pennsylvania, and teaches classes in the Spanish and Core Curriculum departments at Eastern Mennonite University (EMU), Harrisonburg, Virginia. He has graduate degrees from Wichita State University (Spanish literature), Wichita, Kansas; and Eastern Mennonite Seminary (Spiritual Formation), Harrisonburg. Prior to EMU, he taught Spanish, German, and Core Curriculum classes. He led the Global Issues Seminar at Hesston College, Kansas. He was director of Cross-Cultural Programs at Eastern Mennonite University and worked as Director of Communications at Virginia Mennonite Missions and Virginia Mennonite Conference.

Clymer spent years processing his intercultural experiences in Central America and Mexico where he worked with Eastern Mennonite Missions, Salunga, Pennsylvania, and Mennonite Central Committee, Akron, Pennsylvania, and where he studied and led numerous student groups. His journey gives him significant insight and passion for connecting spirituality and the cross-cultural experience.

Clymer is married to Esther Reichenbach, a native of Switzerland, and has two adult children. Don and Esther are members of Lindale Mennonite Church, Linville, Virginia, where Don has served as elder, worship leader, song leader, and Sunday school teacher as well as being on the pastoral care team.

www.ingramcontent.com/pod-product-compliance
Lightning Source LLC
Chambersburg PA
CBHW022108040426
42451CB00007B/182